My Life Cycle

My Life as an
EMPEROR
PENGUIN

PICTURE WINDOW BOOKS
a capstone imprint

Published by Picture Window Books, an imprint of Capstone
1710 Roe Crest Drive, North Mankato, Minnesota 56003
capstonepub.com

Library of Congress Cataloging-in-Publication Data is available on the Library of Congress website
ISBN: 9781663984845 (hardcover)
ISBN: 9781666332773 (ebook PDF)

Summary: Hi, there! I'm an emperor penguin. I might be the largest penguin on Earth, but I started life much smaller, just like you! Learn more about my life cycle and how I went from an egg to the king of Antarctica.

Editorial Credits
Editor: Alison Deering; Designer: Kay Fraser; Media Researcher: Svetlana Zhurkin;
Production Specialist: Katy LaVigne

My Life as an EMPEROR PENGUIN

by John Sazaklis

illustrated by Doc Nguyen

Welcome to Antarctica! I am an emperor penguin, and this is my empire. You may call me your majesty!

Just kidding! I'm not really royalty.

My family and I are called emperor penguins because we are the biggest penguins alive today. We can stand up to 4 feet (122 centimeters) tall and weigh as much as 100 pounds (45 kilograms)!

EMPEROR PENGUIN

KING PENGUIN

ROYAL PENGUIN

5

I didn't start off this large and in charge. First, I was a cute and cuddly egg.

Back then, I only measured about 5 inches (13 cm) long. I was a lightweight too. Emperor penguin eggs weigh a little less than 1 pound (0.5 kg).

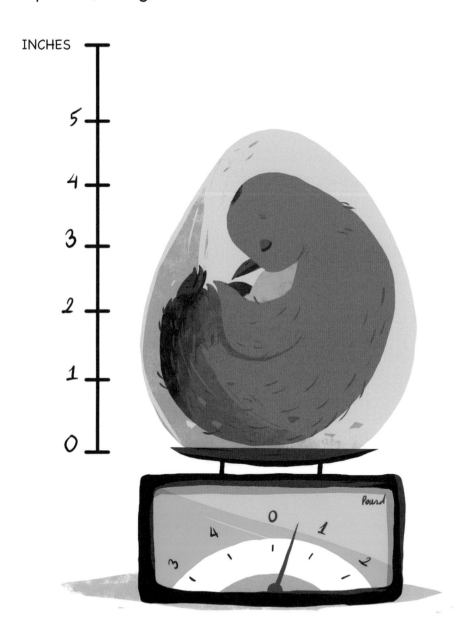

Have you ever seen such an expressive baby? The camera loves me!

Emperor penguins lay a single egg at a time, usually in May or June. Unfortunately, that's right before winter starts in Antarctica. It can drop to minus 120 degrees Fahrenheit (minus 84 degrees Celsius). **BRRR!**

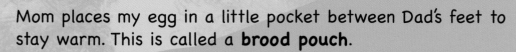

Mom places my egg in a little pocket between Dad's feet to stay warm. This is called a **brood pouch**.

With me safe and sound, Mom takes off for an "egg-citing" two-month adventure in the ocean to find food. She's one hungry hunter!

Meanwhile, Dad does an "egg-cellent" job of keeping my egg nice and warm—and off the snow. He calls this period of bonding **incubation**. But I have to break free!

After about 65 days, it's time to hatch. It takes me a few days to crack out of the egg. I use my beak to push against the shell until it breaks. **CRACK!**

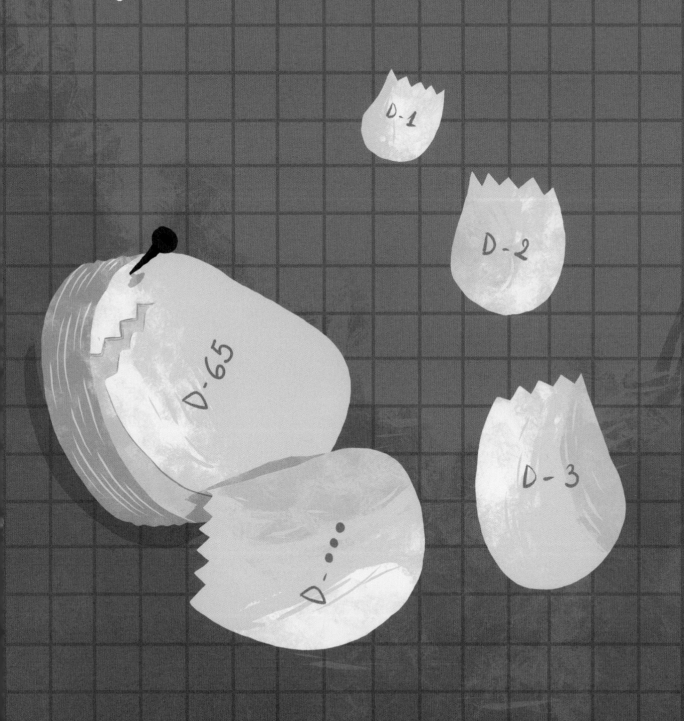

Now I'm a baby penguin—also known as a chick! As a chick, I have a fluffy coat of gray and brown feathers called **down**. It is not only fashionable—it's functional! This coat keeps me warm when the temperature drops.

Thankfully, we live in a group called a **colony**. The grown-ups and the chicks huddle together to stay warm. And with 5,000 penguins—or more—it's a big huddle!

I'm starving, and Mom isn't back with food yet. But Dad's got a brilliant idea. He's gonna upchuck some fatty milk from inside his throat and feed it to me. *Yum!*

I'm not the only one who's hungry. Dad hasn't eaten since he arrived at the colony. He's lost almost half his body weight. Trust me, you wouldn't like him when he's *hangry!*

Finally, at the beginning of August, Mom returns. Dad lets out a special call so she knows where we are, but he doesn't want to share me . . . yet!

Mom brought us **krill**, squid, and fish. Rub-a-dub-dub, let's get this grub!

My parents eat 4 to 7 pounds (2 to 3 kg) of food a day. They chew up the food and feed it to me until I'm older.

Once Mom is back, Daddy duty is over. He heads for the ocean, and Mom takes charge. But after about a month and a half, it's time for me to experience some independence.

I hop down from Mom's feet to go hang with the other chicks. It will be five months before we learn to swim and hunt on our own. So, for now, we huddle together in a small group called a **crèche** to keep warm. I hope no one has bad breath!

During my group hang time, I grow a lot. I also begin to **molt**. This is a very embarrassing time for me. I look like someone decided to play Pin the Feathers on the Penguin and ran out of feathers! EEK!

20 INCHES

15

10

5

0

Eventually my down coat is replaced with two layers of sleek, waterproof feathers. I even have feathers on my legs, so my ankles don't freeze! They are black and white, like a tuxedo. I am always ready for a formal party!

Just because I'm a bird, it doesn't mean I can fly. Instead of wings, emperor penguins have flippers and webbed feet.

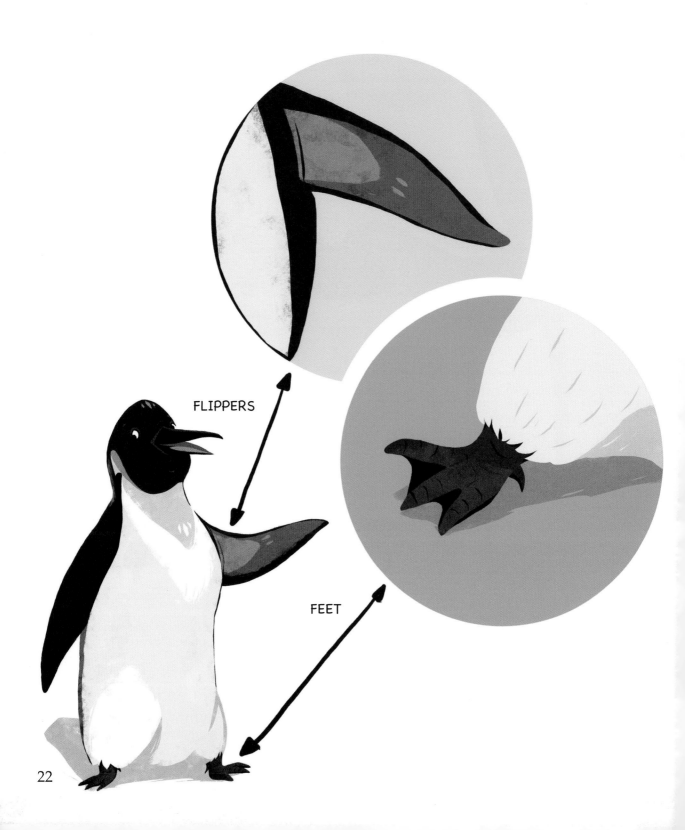

FLIPPERS

FEET

But don't feel too bad—I might waddle on land, but in the water, I am an Olympic-level swimmer! I can dive as deep as 1,850 feet (564 meters). And I can stay underwater for more than 20 minutes. Give me that gold medal!

It takes two to three years, but I finally grow big and
tall. As an adult penguin, I am about the same height as
a 6-year-old child.

My feathers are still black and white, but I've got some color in my life . . . areas of orange and yellow on my head, neck, and beak!

I split my time between the colony and the ocean. I also keep an eye out for **predators**. Leopard seals might make a meal out of me, and I want to live to the ripe old age of 20!

In a few years, it'll be time for me to pair up and make an egg of my own. My parents will be proud emperor grand-penguins . . . and the circle of life continues!

My Life as an Emperor Penguin

About the Author

John Sazaklis is a *New York Times* bestselling author with more than 100 children's books under his utility belt! He has also illustrated Spider-Man books, created toys for *MAD* magazine, and written for the *BEN 10* animated series. John lives in New York City with his superpowered wife and daughter.

About the Illustrator

Duc Nguyen was born and raised in Ho Chi Minh City, Vietnam, and earned a bachelor's degree in graphic design and illustration from Ho Chi Minh City University of Fine Arts. Duc started her career at a local magazine and has gained experience working on a variety of books for many domestic and foreign publishers. In her spare time, Duc loves baking, creating handmade items, and spending time with her dogs.

Glossary

brood pouch (BROOD PAUCH)—a hollow sack on an animal where eggs develop

colony (KAH-luh-nee)—a large group of animals that live together in the same area

crèche (KRESH)—a group of young animals (such as penguins) gathered in one place for care and protection, usually by one or more adults

down (DOWN)—the soft, fluffy feathers of a bird

incubation (in-kyuh-BAY-shuhn)—sitting on eggs and keeping them warm so they hatch

krill (KRIL)—a small, shrimplike animal

molt (MOHLT)—to shed feathers; after molting, a new layer of feathers grows

predator (PRED-uh-tur)—an animal that hunts other animals for food

Index